WAKE UP AMERICA,
OUR CHILDREN ARE DYING!

MICHELLE VERA, M.D.

TABLE OF CONTENTS

DEDICATION

"A voice is heard in Ramah, mourning and great weeping, Rachel weeping for her children and refused to be comforted, because her children are no more. This is what the Lord says: Restrain your voice from weeping and your eyes from tears, for your work will be rewarded; declares the Lord. They will return from the land of the enemy." 1 This book is dedicated to women everywhere who are crying out for help for their troubled children. They do not know what to do and do not know where to turn for help. There is help!

1 The New King James Bible, Jeremiah 31: 15,16.

ACKNOWLEDGMENT

My special thanks to the Lord and His word that never fails and never returns void. I want to thank my wonderful husband, my children and my family and friends who loved me and encouraged me during the most difficult time of my life. I want to thank my husband, Eric, who always loves me; Betty who allowed me to be a part of her life sharing her anguish so I may be a source of help for her. Nehemiah who had the courage and tenacity to never give up; Cristina who plays the piano like an angel and always lifts my spirit up; and Danielle with her special hugs and kisses that keep me going throughout the day. Pastor Don and Norma who prayed for me, when I did not know how to pray, and Pastor Everett and Ruth who believed that I was strong, when I felt so weak and so many other people who loved me through this difficult time of my life. Names were changed to protect identity.

CHAPTER 1

His Testimony

Now to Him who is able to do exceedingly abundantly above all that we ask or think, according to the power that works in us, to Him be glory in the church by Christ Jesus to all generations, forever and ever. Amen.

Ephesians 3:20, 21 New King James Bible

This chapter was written by our best friend's son, Nehemiah. I have included his paper entitled "Success" in my book, allowing you to read his point of view about what happened to us, as well as to get to know him better. His insight into success in life, determination, and courage is an inspiration to me, and I hope to you.

Success: There are many different kinds of success. Success can be small or large. It can change your life in dramatic ways in which you will never be the same. According to Webster, success is a favorable or desired outcome. There are certain aspects in which certain people succeed in and in most cases people who succeed have started at a very low place or even in a state of failure. This is true in my case. I am successful in football, but more importantly in life. This is the story of my success both on and off the field.

There were two sides to my life before I came into a relationship with a person that changed it. My first life was a life full of selfishness, sorrow and revelry. I started drinking and toying with drugs when I was thirteen year's old and in eighth grade. I was always educated and warned about the harmful effects that take place when using drugs and drinking too much alcohol. Nevertheless, I started on the account of my desire to be accepted and cool. I started out smoking tobacco and marijuana and drinking occasionally. This however changed extremely quickly.

My party habit, that was once a rare social occasion, started becoming an everyday occurrence. My grades soon started to drop along with my desire to play sports and get involved with athletics. Soon I would even lose my interest in the opposite sex because of my obsession with alcohol, going to the extent of choosing a beer over hanging with my girlfriend.

By the time spring of my eighth-grade year came around, my alcohol habit nearly killed me. I was hanging out with some older kids from high school on a Sunday afternoon and I ended up getting into a drinking contest with one of the biggest alcoholics in the school. I remember being angry that I only got to drink one time that weekend, so to make up for it, I felt I had to really overdo it on that day. Within an hour, I had drank ten beers and finished off half a fifth of peppermint schnapps hard liquor. Immediately after this fiasco, I was driven home drunk as a skunk. My parents had never noticed or suspected me of drinking or doing any drugs before this time.

My whole life since the beginning of the year had been a lie. After throwing up blood and every other thing in my system, in the bath room for two hours passed out, I woke with a knock from my mother, that it was time for dinner. This time I couldn't hang on or put on a fake personality and façade to hide my problem. I managed to trip down the hall, running into everything on the way there, just to pass out again this time face flat in my pillow. My mother soon came up wondering what was taken so long to find her first born son half dead and reeking of alcohol. She immediately went hysterical and dragged me to the hospital screaming obscenities at me the whole ride over. Meanwhile, I was in and out of consciousness the whole way there and in the waiting room of the ER. The doctors said that I had blown a 1.7 on the blood alcohol level after a four to five hour wait before being found and taken to the hospital. Medically, I was told that I could have easily slipped into a coma and died. Yet, I walked out of the hospital later only having put sufficient damage on my liver.

This incident of course didn't invoke any warning flashes that I might have a problem with alcohol or that I might be living my life recklessly. After a long tormenting four weeks of being sober and grounded, I went out and got plastered the first night I was allowed out of the house. After my mother found out about my drinking through the hospital incident, she hired a private detective to follow me around. He later brought evidence of my partying and other habits to the attention of my mother, which in turn drove her to a form of insanity.

During my eighth-grade summer, I also encountered a rare phenomenon that I thought non-existent. I had what I learned to be demons attacking me. In reality, I was being harassed. My bed would shake constantly through the night, every night, and not just when I would sit on it, but when my family would sit on it as well. I would also have my light flicker and click by itself along with shadows constantly changing form on my walls into different shapes and animals. I would also have terrifying dreams when I could finally get to sleep. There would also be extremely loud pounding on the garage door on occasion. It sounded like someone was pounding a sledge hammer on the door. Yet when my dad would go out to check to see who was doing this there would be no one to see. These scary occurrences would freeze my every muscle fiber in my body until I couldn't move or make a sound. Some people think that demons are fiction and are not real. I, for one, was one of these people before I had encounters with them. Little did I know that I invited them in unknowingly by hiding a switchblade with the inscription black magic on the knife. Later, after lots of prayer on behalf of my mother and all her friend's part, they left. Yet all this, and I still was completely lost and still felt a feeling that I was invincible.

My freshman year came and left filled with many problems with my family and the law. With my drinking came a rage within me I never knew existed. I would be filled with rage and hate toward my parents and everything my parents did and said. They would try to help me stop my drinking and I would be furious. They would try to ground me for getting drunk and I would let my wrath out on them. A couple of times I got physical with them and they called the cops on me. I would then leave for hours, running from the police and building an even bigger barrier between my family and I.

My ninth-grade summer was filled with even more drinking. This time, I drank because of the problems I was having at home, and ironically, my problems at home were caused by my drinking. This summer I would wake up, go to my friend's house and get plastered, and then later go out at night and get plastered. I would often wake up drinking screwdrivers and go to bed taking shots of Bacardi 151.

During the course of the year, my friends' parents tried every form of help available to help me with my alcoholism as well as my anger problem. I would go to a psychologist, psychiatrist, AA meetings and drug rehab centers. All of these forms of professional help, and I still couldn't stop drinking or even admit that I was an alcoholic in the first place. Soon at the end of that summer, my family decided to move us to New Mexico.

My first Sunday there I was dragged to a local church just like every other Sunday of my life. This Sunday, the pastor asked all the youth to come up to the front to get prayed for. So, I went up to receive prayer and nothing happened. The next week the same events occurred. I slept and woke up as the pastor called all the youth up again to be prayed for. Just like the last Sunday I went up got prayer and nothing happened. Finally, on September 15, 1999, I went to church again as usual. This time I my gaze was preoccupied by a black man that walked in with a huge afro, big thick, black square glasses, and dressed in a plaid green seventies suit with bellbottoms. I found out later that no one had ever seen this man before in there church, and I definitely had never seen this man before in my life. The man was dancing and praising Jesus like a total fool. Hollering, and jumping up and down and dancing. The man eventually made his way up to the front and took the microphone from the pastor and called up the youth again to be prayed for.

At this point in time I had had enough of getting up to be prayed for, but nonetheless, I got up and walked to the front. This time around was different. The black man who had taken control of the service immediately passed everyone and came directly over to me. He started praying for me in a loud tone and then started telling me my whole life story. He not only told me my life, but in detail. He knew things about me that my parents didn't even know and yet I had never met this person in my life. I knew that the power of satan was real after my encounter in eighth grade, but I never really experienced the power and realism that Jesus Christ showed me on that day through this man that I had never seen or met before in my life.

After hearing my whole life of sin regurgitated back to me in what seemed like an hour, yet was in reality five minutes, I dropped to my knees and gave my life over to Christ. Immediately after he told me this he walked right out of the church and no one ever saw him again. Even the man who met this guy the night before at a fair, and who let him stay over at his house, and gave him a ride to church never saw him again.

After this experience, I was never the same again. I gave up my drinking and wild irresponsible life and took on a new one full of success and prosperity. I soon moved into the next phase in my life; football, and got my priorities straightened out. I started playing football when I was about seven or eight years old. I would play almost every day in the neighborhood after school and every day at recess at school. Most of my friends at school were all signed up in peewee football leagues by the time I was in fourth grade. I would ask my mom every year if I could play but she would always give me the same answer of, "Why don't you choose another sport that is less injury prone?" As you may be able to tell, my mother was not a big fan of me playing football. Of course I wasn't even heavy enough to make the varsity squad when I was that age. The weight class was 89-112 pounds in 4th grade and I couldn't even make the weight.

Time continued to pass and I played all other organized sports while I was growing older and bigger. When I got to 7th grade, my mom let me try out for the football team and the weight cut off was 100 pounds this time. I failed to make weight and could not make the team. Like all other obstacles in my life, this of course never stopped me. I just ate more and that summer I got a little help from a 7-inch growth spurt and

40-pound weight gain to go with it. I was now about 5'10 130 pounds and I was ready to play this year.

When I got out on the field with my pads for the first time, it was an amazing feeling. I loved every minute of it. From the time we stretched to the end of team scrimmages I was absorbed and taken up in the sport. I started my first season riding the bench during my 8th grade season. I wasn't good enough to make the first string that year, but I set goals and took byte size pieces and not only accomplished my goal of making first string on one side of the ball but both. I started my freshman year out at wide receiver and outside linebacker.

That year I found my passion in life; playing linebacker. Although I lost my job in the middle of the year to a bigger kid and got moved to cornerback, that didn't stop me. I just set goals of getting bigger, and stronger, and making it at linebacker next year. By next season I had grown to 6'0 feet tall and weighed around 170 pounds. Hitting the weight room hard during the winter really helped a lot. My sophomore year I didn't get to start on varsity. I was a second string behind a senior. I learned a lot that season and it helped me be the player that I am today. At the end of this season I also set goals to gain more weight, get stronger, and start at linebacker next year. So one year later I was 185 pounds and I was starting at middle linebacker. After an ok season as a junior I decided that one more year of football for my life wasn't long enough. Just like I had done in every other season in my life, I set goals. This time it was to play for a Division I A college after my senior season. My senior season I came in at 6'1 205 pounds and by the end of the season I had over 100 tackles, 3 forced fumbles, 3 sacks, and one interception. This season was good enough to win best defensive player of the year, all-state honors, and all-conference honors. After my season was over, I sent out video tape all over the place and only got recruited by a couple of smaller division schools. I had done everything in my power to get recruited by top schools and yet I did not get offers. Still I did not give up.

After almost losing all hopes of playing college football, I decided that I would try to get into the schools academically first and then send my video in. Finally I achieved my goal with the hand of God moving me into the right place at the right time in the first week of February. All my hard work paid off; I made it to University of Alabama. The choice from there was easy, big ten football with great academics. My goal setting still did not come to a close though. Instead, it had just begun. I had to work harder in the off-season that year than in all the other years put together. I started by setting goals like always. I wanted to weigh 220 pounds, run between a 4.5-4.7 forty time, and bench over 300 pounds.

After training six days a week from December through August my dream came into full view. I currently weigh 220, run a 4.6 forty, and bench 315 pounds. All my hard work finally became worthwhile. I am currently on the University of Alabama football team and by setting goals, and putting my trust in God, I accomplished more than I ever could hope, dream, or imagine. Success in my life did not ever come easy. I struggled through many trials and circumstances. With the help of God and determination and hard work I have become a successful man. I have made it to the place where I am in a desired or favorable outcome not just in football, but in life as well. I started off as a failure and at a very low place. But it doesn't matter where you start in a race, it's where you finish is what matters.

CHAPTER 2

My Testimony

"I waited patiently for God to help me; then he listened and heard my cry. He lifted me out of the pit of despair, out from the bog and the mire, and set my feet on a hard, firm path, and steadied me as I walked along. He has given me a new song to sing, of praises to our God.

Now many will hear of the glorious things he did for me, and stand in awe before the Lord, and put their trust in him."

Psalm 40:1-3 New King James Bible

I am writing this testimony today in the hope of possibly saving just one tear, or giving one mother new hope, or helping one adolescent on the road to recovery and freedom in Christ. I am a Christian, Family Physician and mother of three children, ages 18, 15 and 13. My husband is a Christian Obstetrician/Gynecologist. Betty and I had families that, amid the normal chaotic life we led, we thought that we had managed to keep our lives in good control. Although our homes were certainly not perfect, we felt that we were able to balance our Christian values, educational goals and family time. I worked part-time as a physician keeping my schedule free in the afternoons. We attended a great charismatic church in the area, and our children were busy with the usual soccer, piano, baseball, friends, etc. I tried to make up for the hectic schedule my husband kept as an Obstetrician/ Gynecologist by being available in the afternoons. I was taxi driver, cook etc. in the afternoons, and doctor by day. We went to church on Sundays, and sometimes on Wednesdays, read the Bible occasionally, and prayed together as a family. Betty homeschooled her children for a while and then put her children into the public system while she returned to work as a teacher.

In April 1998, an event occurred that changed all our lives. My best friend, Betty and her son Nehemiah who lived nearby were visiting us for the day. We had been like sisters and shared everything for over 15 years. When we returned to her home on that Sunday afternoon, I felt uneasiness inside and was determined to sit on the couch until her son arrived home. There was really no reason to worry as Nehemiah had gone to the movies with a friend Saul, two years older than he and we knew that he was safe. Saul was a model student and we felt that he protected her son.

When the two of them arrived home, Nehemiah went up to the bathroom while Saul went outside to play basketball. It seemed like a long time as I sat patiently on the couch feeling that there was nothing that could convince me to leave this couch until I saw Nehemiah face-to-face. Certainly, there was plenty to do around the house to help get dinner ready, but the uneasiness I felt would not allow me to move from the family room couch,

After forty-five minutes, Saul came inside and I told him to check on Nehemiah, because he had been in the bathroom for a long time. Saul checked on him and he said, "Something is wrong with Nehemiah!" and told me to come upstairs to the room where Nehemiah was. I cannot explain the terror that I felt when I saw Nehemiah on his bed so drunk that he could not talk. Thoughts of alcohol mixed with drugs filled my mind; I feared that he would suddenly stop breathing right in front of me, and I would have to perform CPR right there. Fearing for his life, Betty, Saul and I grabbed him and somehow got him into our car and drove him to the hospital. I thought that it would be faster than waiting for an ambulance because we lived five minutes away. At the emergency room, he was given IV fluids quickly and responded well. When he awoke, he told us that this was the first time he had ever drunk alcohol and that I was overreacting.

This event began the many months of soul-searching and crying out to the Lord, to try to determine why I had not realized that Nehemiah had such a problem with alcohol. OR why I had not known that he was drinking alcohol. I had thought that I was doing a good balancing act of being a doctor, mother, cook, chauffeur, wife and Christian. How had this drinking escaped me? If anyone should have been able to catch Nehemiah's drinking alcohol before this episode occurred, it should have been me. I had all the medical training; I was available in the afternoons and I grew up with parents who were alcoholics. I struggled with the question of what I was going to do next to help my best friend's son and their family get through this. My friend was unable to cope, frozen in space, ready for a nervous breakdown. She begged me to take over. I felt that I was the only hope. So many people said, "All kids go through that. After all, we were worse when we grew up." Or, "Oh, he is a good kid and will come around." I felt like I was fighting for his life and the world was telling me that I was just too serious, that I was just worried about nothing. I did not feel at peace or reassured with their comments, but rather a constant tremendous anxiety.

Many times, I would wake up in the middle of the night to pray for Nehemiah.

We tried everything available! We brought him to a few different secular psychologists, a Christian psychologist, and attended workshops at the public high school about how to deal with difficult or strong-willed youth. Nehemiah, his Dad and I even attended a rehabilitation clinic group session held nightly, once a week for a month. We were told that there was little hope for change because of his poor attitude. He liked the way he was and did not want to change.

I reached out to everyone to pray for Nehemiah. I called friends at many different churches and asked them to pray. I called CBN and many other Christian groups on television to put Nehemiah on every prayer list that I could find. I invited friends and Pastors to come to his room to pray with us. I tried everything I could think of, as well as all of the recommendations from family and friends including going to his room and anointing it with oil, and playing Christian radio in his room all day.

There was nothing quick about this process. I read every book on the occult and prayer while driving the kids around and working part-time. I read two or three books each week, searching for an answer to help Nehemiah. I started my day crying out to the Lord as I walked two to three miles on my treadmill, for the knowledge to know what to do. As I look back, I know it was the Lord helping me to fight all odds. Then, as the Lord began to answer my prayers, I realized the battle was too great to do alone. I definitely needed more help.

My husband and I felt our friends needed to make a big change! They decided to move to another state with a new job to give a new start for Nehemiah. They moved to New Mexico where we were living. They found out that the Lord had some new plans for every one of them in their family as well as us, not just Nehemiah. Through an old friend, who was a Pastor in New Mexico, they established themselves in this area. Nehemiah had an incredible experience while attending a Vineyard Church in New Mexico!

A man visiting the church for the first time called the youth forward to pray for them. This man who had never met Nehemiah before, told him his whole life story. He told Nehemiah details about his life that only Nehemiah knew. Then he told him to repent and surrender his life to the Lord, which is exactly what he did! This began his new life with the Lord and a real purpose for his life. He writes about this in the chapter: His Testimony.

The Lord has done more than we ever hoped or asked for, just as the Bible states. We saw Nehemiah not only turn his life completely around and give up alcohol, but share his testimony with others about the greatness of the Lord. However, the Lord did more than that. Nehemiah was selected all-state linebacker in 2001 for his football division, and was asked to be a "walk on" for Alabama State University and the University of Alabama football teams. He was accepted to Alabama State University as a "walk on" to play for the football team the year they became division champions. Academically, he was successful in being admitted to the Alabama State University, Florida State University, University of Alabama and many other schools. We were thrilled to see supernatural changes in Nehemiah through the hand of the Lord.

Along the way, I gathered information to share with others regarding prayer, medical aspects, communication skills, common sense approaches, and basic biblical principles. This self-help book is written to encourage and teach you how to help your own children out of drugs, alcohol, broken relationships, and problem lifestyles. The Bible states that, "My people perish for lack of knowledge."—We need knowledge to take back what the enemy has stolen—our children.

CHAPTER 3

Let's Take Inventory

And you will know the truth,
And the truth will set you free.

John 8:32 The New Living Bible

Sometimes I felt afraid to find out the truth. I had a feeling that something was wrong, but I could not put my finger on it. I thought maybe Nehemiah was going through the "rebellious teenager stage" and that he would be fine so I should not worry. That is what many people told me and I wanted to believe them. Something inside me told me that there was a real problem and I had to find out what it was. Do not be afraid of the truth about your teenager "for the truth will set you free."

There are many authors and respected counselors all over the country sending a message to parents that their adolescents are going through a normal stage of "rebellion." They state that adolescents need to go through this stage in order to grow into healthy adults. The emphasis is that, "we all went through this stage and survived," and that parents just need to, "make sure that their teens do not get too out of hand with drinking and drugs." I am in complete disagreement with this idea. The consumption of alcohol and drugs has led to many other problems—drunk drivers, teen pregnancy, sexually transmitted diseases in epidemic proportions, and even the transmission of Aids. Alcohol and drugs cloud the teenager's minds, decreasing their inhibitions and thus making it hard to, "Just say No!" when asked to participate in activities that they would otherwise not participate in. Peer pressure also encourages these illicit activities and soon they drift off into a path and pattern to destroy their lives.

The adolescents are crying out to us so we can recognize that they need our help desperately. They need the 1960's parents of the hippie era to wake up. The massacre in Colorado at Columbine High School was just the beginning. This is a very important sign that we all need to change both as Christian parents and non-Christian parents alike.

The following is a list of signs and symptoms of children who use drugs and alcohol obtained from a rehabilitation treatment center for teenagers involved in substance abuse. The list was written by the Rehabilitation Center to make parents more aware of what to look for in their child if they are worried that their children may be using drugs or alcohol. Most of the items in this list are describing someone with a very serious drug or alcohol abuse. Start asking a lot of questions if you find these items present in your adolescent. Also, it is important to look for changes in behavior regarding relationship to parents, siblings, grades in school, sports activities, new friends, especially when the behavior identified is different from a year ago or so.

Signs and Symptoms of Chemical Dependence List:

1. Increase in the amount of alcohol or other drugs used.
2. Arrested for MIP (minor in possession) offense.
3. Dramatic change in mood when drinking or using.
4. Denial of any problem.
5. Dishonesty with peers about drinking or using.

6. Failed attempts to quit or cut down on chemical use.
7. Association with known heavy users.
8. Frequent excuses for chemical use.
9. Protecting supply of chemicals.
10. Low self-image.
11. Hangovers or bad trips.
12. School suspension, especially if this is for chemical use.
13. Frequent mood changes or isolation from family members.
14. Deterioration of school grades.
15. Stealing money.
16. Using chemicals while alone.
17. Loss of control especially if done while using or drinking.
18. Health problems.
19. Suicidal thoughts or behaviors.
20. Dropped by girlfriend or boyfriend because of chemical use.
21. Violent behavior especially if high or drunk.
22. Preoccupation with chemicals.
23. Increase in the frequency of chemical use.
24. Increase in tolerance, i.e. drinking more each week to get drunk.
25. Memory loss.
26. Using chemicals in the morning.
27. Loss of friends.
28. Frequent broken promises.
29. Defensive when confronted.
30. Fired from jobs.

Actually, I felt that I did not need to read this list of behaviors to think this teenager was in trouble. I had this gut feeling that something was not right. I saw there were significant changes in his personality, a change in his grades, and increasing arguments with his family at home. We suspected that he was drinking alcohol and / or taking drugs. Have you felt that way or entertained thoughts like these? But what do you do now? What do you do if you think there is something wrong?

When Betty, my husband and I confronted Nehemiah, arguments and problems increased with breakdown in communication afterwards. He told us that everything was, "fine", and that we were just, "nosey" or, "paranoid." Then this would usually result in an argument about who is right rather than resolving anything. Nehemiah was very angry for a day or two with all of us.

I was searching for the truth. Are you searching for the truth? How can you find out the truth? And what can you do when you find the truth to help your children? I hope that this book can give you some of the answers to these questions.

Section D: chemical Dependence Information, signs and symptoms of chemical dependence list.

QUESTIONS

After reading this chapter, stop for a moment and consider the following questions. Then use the space to write out some of your feelings. What do you feel is the major problem in your life and whom does it involve? Do you suspect that you have a son or daughter that is involved with drugs or alcohol?

CHAPTER 4

Why Me, Lord? Help Me to Understand!

Why Me, Lord? Help Me Understand! I waited patiently for God to help me; then He listened and heard my cry. He lifted me out of the pit of despair, out from the bog and the mire, and set my feet on a hard, firm path, and steadied me as I walked along. He has given me a new song to sing, of praises to our God. Now many will hear of the glorious things He did for me, and stand in awe before the Lord, and put their trust in Him. Many blessings are given to those who trust the Lord.

Psalm 40:1-3 The Living Bible

When I discovered that Nehemiah had been drinking alcohol and taking drugs without my knowledge for quite a while, my first thought was, "Why me? How did this happen? What did I do wrong?" I cried out to the Lord and asked, "Why me, Lord?!" I wondered why the Lord would have desired to test in this way, and why was the devil after Nehemiah's life? Our families attended church regularly, followed the Ten Commandments, as well as read the Bible once in a while. We even went to

Wednesday night service a few times a month. Overall, we thought that we were pretty good Christians. I decided to search the Bible for some answers to my questions and found some helpful bible verses. I wanted to find the cause of his problem, so I could fix it.

In the book of the Bible called Exodus, Chapter 16 verse 4, the Bible states, *"Then the Lord said to Moses, 'Behold, I will rain bread from heaven for you. And the people shall go out and gather a certain quota every day, that I may test them whether they will walk in my law or not.'"* I realized after reading this passage of scripture, that sometimes our difficult situations are the result of the Lord testing us. He wants to see if we will truly follow Him and obey His laws even when our life is not easy. The book of Job in the Bible is another example of a life that was not easy, but the Lord blessed him with more children and material wealth after the testing than before.

Of course, Nehemiah's decisions were more complicated than that because they also involved the consequences of very poor decisions. There is another Bible verse which describes this:

> *Be not deceived; God is not mocked: for whatsoever a man soweth, that shall he also reap.*
> Gal 6:7 KJV Bible Version

God is not mocked as you read in this verse. A person will reap what he or she sows. Nehemiah was reaping what he had been sowing. His poor choices resulted in poor consequences. As I searched further, I found that there were additional scriptures regarding the testing of the Lord.

Another scripture that describes this is found in Exodus, Chapter 20 verse 18. In this passage of scripture, the Lord has just given the Ten Commandments to the Israelites who are living in the desert:

> *"Now all the people witnessed the thundering, and lightning flashes, and the sound of the trumpet, and the mountain smoking: and when the people saw it, they trembled and stood afar off. Then they said to Moses, 'you speak with us and we will hear, but let not God speak with us, lest we die'. And Moses said to the people, 'Do not fear: for God has come to test you, and that his fear may be before you, so that you may not sin.'"* The New King James Bible, Exodus 20:18.

It was clear that sometimes we need to be reminded of the "fear of the Lord" so that we may not sin. This is the reverence or respect for the Lord. This respect for the Lord provokes in us a desire to obey Him. It is similar to when you were a small child and your father had to remind you how important it was to obey him. As children we did not always agree with the punishment or rules, but a good speaking to or spanking got our attention and we had a new respect for our parents.

God allows many situations in our lives to test us, prove us, or remind us about the importance of obedience. The Bible refers to the fact that there will be many tribulations for us and not all of them are from God. The Lord promises to take us through our problems, not remove them.

Temptations, on the other hand are from the devil. "Let no one say when he is tempted, "I am tempted by God"; for God cannot be tempted by evil, nor does He Himself tempt anyone. But each one is tempted when he is drawn away by his own desires and enticed. Then when desire has conceived, it gives birth to sin; and sin, when it is full-grown, brings forth death."

The Lord may also allow difficult situations to occur, or the situations may occur due to our disobedience, in order to change our character. This is what God is really after—our character. The book of the Bible called James, chapter one explains this: *"My brethren, count it all joy when you fall into various trials, knowing that the testing of your faith produces patience. But let patience have its perfect work so that you may be perfect and complete, lacking nothing."*

As our character is perfected through the development of patience, then we will not lack anything. This process is not very easy for me as I find it difficult to always be joyful when I am going through problems. However, I am learning to depend on the Lord for my peace trusting in Him, rather than depending on my circumstances to give me peace. Our circumstances will change, but the Lord does not change. He is the same yesterday, today and forever.

In researching the Bible for the answers to my problem, I looked for possible causes for the onslaught of problems that we were encountering, so I could change the circumstances. The circumstances got my attention!! I had thought that being a Christian was easy. Disobedience was one topic that I studied. Although I had memorized the Ten Commandments as a child and believed that I followed them; I was surprised upon reviewing the contents. I realized that if I followed the Ten Commandments, then I was blessed and if I did not follow them, then I would be cursed. Simple. The Lord is a God of covenant, meaning that He always follows through with his promises which are written in the Bible. Read the scriptures for yourself and see which side you are on—the blessings or the curses.

Exodus 20

1 *"Then God issued this edict:"*

2 *"I am Jehovah your God who liberated you from your slavery in Egypt."*

3 *"You may worship no other god than me."*

4 *"You shall not make yourselves any idols: no images of animals, birds, or fish."*

5 *"You must never bow or worship it in any way; for I, the Lord your God, am very possessive. I will not share your affection with any other god!" "And when I punish people for their sins, the punishment continues upon the children, grandchildren, and great-grandchildren of those who hate me;*

6 *"But I lavish my love upon thousands of those who love me and obey my commandments."*

7 *"You shall not use the name of Jehovah your God irreverently, nor use it to swear to a falsehood. You will not escape punishment if you do."*

8 *"Remember to observe the Sabbath as a holy day."*

9 *"Six days a week are for your daily duties and your regular work,"*

10 *"...but the seventh day is a day of Sabbath rest before the Lord your God. On that day you are to do no work of any kind, nor shall your son, daughter, or slaves— whether men or women— or your cattle or your house guests."*

11 *"For in six days the Lord made the heaven, earth, and sea, and everything in them, and rested the seventh day; so he blessed the Sabbath day and set it aside for rest..."*

12 *"Honor your father and mother, that you may have a long, good life in the land the Lord your God will give you."*

13 *"You must not murder."*

14 *"You must not commit adultery."*

15 *"You must not steal."*

16 *"You must not lie…"*

17 *"You must not be envious of your neighbor's house, or want to sleep with his wife, or want to own his slaves, oxen, donkeys, or anything else he has."*

18 *"All the people saw the lightning and the smoke billowing from the mountain, and heard the thunder and the long, frightening trumpet blast; and they stood at a distance, shaking with fear."*

19 *"They said to Moses, 'You tell us what God says and we will obey, but don't let God speak directly to us, or it will kill us.'"*

20 *"Don't be afraid," Moses told them, "for God has come in this way to show you his awesome power, so that from now on you will be afraid to sin against him!"*

Did you notice the end of this last verse that states, *'you will be afraid to sin against him?'* The Lord demonstrated His power in order to make sure the Israelites were afraid to sin against the Lord.

DEUTERONOMY 28

1 *"If you fully obey all of these commandments of the Lord your God, the laws I am declaring to you today, God will transform you into the greatest nation in the world."*

2-6 *"These are the blessings that will come upon you: Blessings in the city, Blessings in the field; Many children, Ample crops, Large flocks and herds; Blessings of fruit and bread;*
Blessings when you come in, Blessings when you go out."

7 *"The Lord will defeat your enemies before you; they will march out together against you but scatter before you in seven directions!"*

8 *"The Lord will bless you with good crops and healthy cattle, and prosper everything you do when you arrive in the land the Lord your God is giving you."*

9 *"He will change you into a holy people dedicated to himself; this he has promised to do if you will only obey him and walk in his ways."*

10 *"All the nations in the world shall see that you belong to the Lord, and they will stand in awe."*

11 *"The Lord will give you an abundance of good things in the land, just as he promised: many children, many cattle, and abundant crops."*

12 *"He will open to you his wonderful treasury of rain in the heavens, to give you fine crops every season. He will bless everything you do; and you shall lend to many nations, but shall not borrow from them."*

13 *"If you will only listen and obey the commandments of the Lord your God that I am giving you today, he will make you the head and not the tail, and you shall always have the upper hand."*

14 *"But each of these blessings depends on your not turning aside in any way from the laws I have given you; and you must never worship other gods."*

15-19 *"If you won't listen to the Lord your God and won't obey these laws I am giving you today, then all of these curses shall come upon you: Curses in the city, Curses in the fields,*

Curses on your fruit and bread, The curse of barren wombs, Curses upon your crops, Curses upon the fertility of your cattle and flocks, Curses when you come in, Curses when you go out."

20 *"For the Lord himself will send his personal curse upon you. You will be confused and a failure in everything you do, until at last you are destroyed because of the sin of forsaking him."*

21 *"He will send disease among you until you are destroyed from the face of the land you are about to enter and possess."*

22 *"He will send tuberculosis, fever, infections, plague, and war. He will blight your crops, covering them with mildew. All these devastations shall pursue you until you perish."*

After reading these biblical verses, I realize that God will honor our obedience to His Word, the Bible. If I refuse to obey God, then curses will follow me. As I obey God, the blessings will overtake me. The studying of the Bible, gave me a greater respect and honor toward the Lord and a greater understanding of what a covenant truly means. This is God's promise to us and we can trust that the Lord will not change. The Lord is not a human being that will fail us. He is God.

If there are areas of your life where you are not following the Lord's instructions or commandments, then I encourage you to stop now and make it right with Him. It is so easy. Just ask him to forgive you and give you His strength to follow Him. There is nothing too big to forgive. He then forgives you and forgets your sin.

QUESTIONS

After reading this chapter, stop for a moment and consider the following questions. Then use the space to write out some of your feelings. **What is the Lord saying to you today? How does this chapter apply to your life? What areas of your life need to be reconciled with the Lord?** Remember that regardless of how big the sin seems to you; the Lord can forgive you.

CHAPTER 5

Tools to Fight the Enemy

Therefore, take up the whole armor of God, that you may be able to withstand in the evil day, and having done all, to stand.

Ephesians 6:13 New King James Bible

STEP 1: NEVER GIVE UP!

I want to advise you about something so vital to the lives of your children: You can never give up! No matter what you see or hear, no matter what your child says to you, you can never give up! Their life may depend on it. And do not be concerned about how long it takes to see a change in your child or the situation. That is the Lord's job, not ours. Just continue believing in the Lord to accomplish the impossible. This is our job. It is very difficult to consistently trust the Lord and be patient with your children while you do not see the changes that you would like to see.

A well-known Christian woman commented one day that her daughter several years ago, had told her mother she did not believe in Jesus Christ while away at college. This shocked me to hear that her daughter had not accepted the Lord as her Savior. The daughter had told her mother that she was searching for the answers to life and was attempting to find the true God through the study of many different religions such as Buddhism, Hinduism, etc. The Christian woman's answer impressed me. She told her daughter that when she returned to give her life to Jesus, her faith would be stronger. This woman still loved her daughter, accepted her and believed in her. She knew that the Lord would be faithful to answer her prayers. She was not moved or affected emotionally by what her daughter had told her.

I admire that kind of faith, that in spite of circumstances which look impossible, she did not give up! What does giving up look like? A friend of mine who is a strong Christian and intercessor (She loves to pray) felt that she should not pray for her son any more, but rather she should just entrust him to the Lord. I struggled with this, because I felt that a mother would be the best person to pray for her son.

Although it is much easier to just turn your children over to God and not to pray for them, I personally do not think that this is God's best. I believe that we should never give up and always expect that God will answer our prayers, but we need to take action—we need a battle plan. Part of this plan is to continue to pray and declare the word of God over our children. I will explain more details of this battle plan in the next few chapters.

Meanwhile, remember to think on the goodness of the Lord rather than your circumstances which may be glaring you in the face. This helps to stop that defeated attitude which brings in depression. *"Finally, brethren whatever things are true, whatever things are noble, whatever things are just, whatever things are pure, whatever things are lovely, and whatever things are of good report, if there is any virtue and if there's anything praiseworthy -- meditate on these things."* Phil. 4:8. It is important to believe that your child will change even when it looks impossible. The Lord is the God of the impossible.

Consider this: How much time do you spend talking to family and friends about all the negative things that your child is doing? How much time do you spend believing in them or in praying for your child? Try changing your lifestyle to spend more time believing in the changes rather than believing in what you see. This is exactly what this Christian woman was doing. By not giving up, she trusted in her prayer to the Lord and the Bible as the basis for this, rather than what her daughter told her.

I discuss this further in the chapter called 'The Word Does Not Return Void'. When you are overwhelmed, or you feel like giving up, call a friend to pray with you. Everyone has moments like that. Remember to, *"Be anxious for nothing, but in everything by prayer and supplication with thanksgiving, let your request be made known to God and the peace of God, which surpasses all understanding will guard your hearts and minds, through Christ Jesus."* Philippians 4:6. In other words, do not be anxious about your problems, but rather pray, ask the Lord for help and then thank Him for answering them. Thank the Lord even if He does not answer you as quickly as you would like.

Another example of being patient in endurance, is when the answer to your prayer is not fulfilled immediately. This is found in the Bible, in the book of Daniel. Daniel had prayed and he had been waiting for his answer. In Daniel, Chapter 10, verse 12, an angel came to him and said: *"Do not fear, Daniel, for from the first day that you set your heart to understand and to humble yourself before your God, your words were heard; and I have come because of your words…"* Our prayers and words are important as well as our patience and faith. It is impossible to please the Lord without faith.

As you can see in the examples above, praying to the Lord is not like ordering at Burger King. You cannot put your prayer request in at the first Burger King window and drive up to the next window to pick-up the answers to your prayer. Our society dictates a lifestyle that is so fast paced that we may expect the Lord to work quickly, and then become discouraged if we do not see results within our expected time frame. Warning: You may need to pray many times per day and wait longer than you would like to. That's OK. Just remember that you can NEVER GIVE UP ON YOUR CHILD!

QUESTIONS

Use this page to write a positive description of how you believe that the Lord would like you to imagine your child. If that is too difficult, then imagine him or her when you use to get along and things worked out well or the way they use to behave when they were younger. Try to replace some of the common negative ways you use to speak to your child with a positive phrase. Write these down now so you can remember them when things get difficult in a disagreement. If you can't think of anything positive to say, tell your child that you are hoping and believing for him/her to change for the better.

STEP 2: GENERAL INFORMATION

Where there is no word from God, people are uncontrolled, but those who obey what they have been taught are happy.

Psalm 29:18 The New Century Bible

This chapter describes some of the practical ideas for you to use on a daily basis to see changes in your family situation. These recommendations are based on spiritual, medical, biblical principles, and common sense. The Lord has given us many tools for fighting off and battling the enemy in order to take back what has been stolen from us - our children, and their heritage. The following are a few practical pointers I would like to briefly comment on, and I hope will be of help. I have also expanded on some of these ideas in other chapters:

1. Prayer

Call your Pastor, or local church, CBN, and every other prayer group available to you. Pray that God will uncover the truth. Once you know the truth, you can begin to know how to pray and believe the Lord to do a miracle.

Next, you can pray the Lord will set your son/daughter free from the enemy. It is the enemy that comes to kill, steal and destroy. This is not the Lord doing this to your child. See my chapter on 'Prayer: Breaking Strongholds', where Dutch Sheets explains more about this subject from his book Intercessory Prayer. Also, read my chapter 8 on 'Prayer that Moves Mountains'.

2. Fast and Pray

Although I do not understand WHY fasting is so powerful, I have seen amazing results. Even skipping breakfast for a week or breakfast and lunch for a few days and then using this time to pray for you child can produce great results. There are many books on fasting. I recommend the book by Dave Williams called 'The Miracle Results of Fasting'. I discuss this further in my chapter on 'Prayer and Fasting'.

3. Remove objects giving Satan glory and not God from your home.

I recommend the book by Chuck Pearce and Rebecca Wagner called "*Ridding your home of Spiritual Darkness*". After studying numerous books on this subject, I have found that there are certain objects that actually invite the devil into your home without your approval or awareness. I have enclosed a portion of this book that enumerates many objects that should be removed in Appendix A. Some of these objects are idols which have been dedicated to the devil in rituals before they are sold to the public. Others, are symbols of the occult which are seen so frequently that you may not even realize what they actually represent.

You can obtain books in the public and Christian bookstores that enumerate the meaning of these symbols. Chuck Pearce writes in his book about his amazing experience in which he removed an occult object he had inadvertently purchased. His wife was free of headaches when the resulting object and spirit left his house. I do not recommend that you remove or break objects belonging to other people without their permission. Nehemiah actually removed some objects himself after being tormented at night with seeing strange pictures on the walls. He was willing to do anything to get a good night's sleep.

4. Free Time

Find out more about who your teenager is spending time with, their siblings and their families. Do not leave them with too much free time that is unaccounted for, especially without adult supervision. Even if the families seem to be the perfect "Leave-It–To-Beaver" family, find out a little more information. I was very surprised to find out what was going on at one of Nehemiah's friend's houses. Although his parents were Christians and frequently attended church, their other son was involved in a lot of other problems. It is important to ask about older siblings and their friends, and what they do in their free time. Attempt to separate your child from the bad influence of friends, if possible. This may be a slow process but remember, do not be misled: *"Bad company corrupts good character."* 1 Corinthians 15:33 NIV Bible Version.

I highly recommend encouraging your child to become involved in a team sport. Sports consume a lot of time and energy, teaches discipline, self-control, and working with others. Look for good role models in their coaches. Additionally, I would warn you that canceling sports is not an area, which I would remove from the daily activities, as a punishment for their bad behavior.

5. Church

Find a church with a great youth group i.e. good music and a fun youth Pastor or Pastors. Do not be afraid to change your church if this is necessary to get your child involved there, even if it is not your first choice. You can find another way to study the Bible or worship, but changing churches may be the most important step you can take for your child. The church may be a way for your child to find another Christian who can help them, either another peer at church or youth leader. Do not allow your children to convince you that all the church activities are boring and stupid and therefore they do not need to go. Tell them to find a youth group that they like, which you also approve of.

6. Counseling Role

I have to say that most of the counselors Nehemiah talked with were a waste of money. And I can assure you that he made sure that we all knew this, too at the time. Look for a Christian counselor who has good values, and search for someone that your child may see as a role model. If your child thinks that the counselor is "stupid", this counselor will not be very useful for him or her. The youth pastor may be helpful. I have found that a role model who is the same sex as your child is more important than the age. - i.e. males listen to males easier and females to females easier. If you do choose a counselor for your child, then make sure to find someone with Christian morals who is able to encourage your child towards the right direction in their decision making.

Counseling has a great reward for both the parents, and children. It is worth the effort for both parents and the child. The counseling can be especially helpful for the mother even if both parents are not available to participate all the time. Just start where you can in your family time constraints. In choosing a counselor, find someone to encourage the parents, and pursue solid Christian values. Also, the counselor should give you some specific direction and tools to help your children.

Additionally, a counselor or youth Pastor can be very helpful when you are emotionally involved with the problems that you are having with your child. There may be a counseling staff at the church you attend that could be helpful for a variety of reasons. The staff could help pray with you individually, or as a family, as well as guide you in difficult decision making and be a support in this difficult time.

7. School

This is your own preference. Nehemiah attended one of the top public schools in the country, which was well known for its academics. It also had almost "90 % to 100%" of the students using alcohol or drugs, according to him. If your child is having problems in the public school, I would definitely look for a private Christian school where your child could have a new start. It is very difficult for anyone to change their behavior while they are living in the same environment, even for adults. Moving Nehemiah out of the environment of the public school and away from his friends was essential for him to be able to change.

I realize that not everyone is able to make a change in which they move out of the area. If you are not able to move out of the area, then seriously consider moving your child to a Christian school. The Christian schools are not perfect either, but they do promote Christian character and values. The peer group at a Christian school is also trying to follow the right way to live and the students are conscious about making mistakes. You may find other situations that you need to adjust, but in balancing everything out, I believe the good outweighs the bad.

8. Parental Agreement

Many wise friends reminded Betty and I repeatedly, that it was essential that we agree in front of our children. If you disagree with your spouse, do not address this in front of your child. This should be discussed in private. It is very important that your child see that you are in unity regarding your decisions in his/her life.

Also be aware that adolescents will try to wear out their parents until they receive the answers that they want to hear. My recommendation is to tell your child to wait until you have an opportunity to discuss any issue with your spouse. This allows you the time to think things out enabling you to make a wise decision and not respond at that moment. In addition, it helps to avoid the child pressuring you with, "Dad (or Mom) said I could do this or that," in order to do what they want to do when the parent did not intend that, or understand the implications. You have a right to say, "Wait. Let me talk to your Dad or Mom."

9. Premenstrual Syndrome and Perimenopause or Menopause.

When the hormones rage in both adolescents and mothers a simple situation can get out of control very quickly. Mothers with PMS (premenstrual syndrome), or premenopausal symptoms (emotional changes occurring around menopause) can aggravate any situation and people overreact to a situation. It seems that these hormones are able to accentuate problems and "build mountains out of mole hills." So, let me address this as both a physician and as a woman.

First, I want you to know that PMS and premenopausal or menopausal symptoms are very real and there are a variety of medications that can help you with this problem, while keeping you in complete control of yourself. Many people do not want to start medications for PMS or Perimenopause or Menopausal symptoms because they believe that they will lose control of themselves. Actually, the opposite is true: You can be in better control of your emotions which is exactly what you need, while taking medications or natural supplements over-the-counter. It can be extremely difficult to have teenagers, with their raging hormones, and women with PMS symptoms, premenopausal or menopausal symptoms in the same house.

If you or your husband feels that this is a possible problem which you are experiencing, then I suggest that you seek the advice of your obstetrician/ gynecologist, or a family doctor. I would like to mention the subject of sleep. Your sleep may be altered as a result of all this stress, confrontations and difficult decisions that have to be made. The result is sleep deprivation which may be a catalyst to result in more problems, and arguments because emotions become out of control on both sides. Please remember it's important to sleep eight hours or so per night without waking up many times in between. Then you're ready to face a new day. There is no need to feel guilty for seeking help in order to address this problem. Everyone in the household will benefit from this. I assure you. It is important for you to know that there are many people taking antidepressants and sleep aids. These medications can be a temporary way to get ahold of the family situation before it gets out of control.

QUESTIONS

Are there medical issues that need to be addressed in order to help your family deal with the problem? Is there someone whether parent or adolescent, with a serious depression that may need medication? Is there a family physician or obstetrician/gynecologist who may be able to help with some of these issues?

STEP 3: CHANGE ME, OH LORD

Change Me, Oh Lord Create in me a clean heart, O God. Renew a right spirit within me. Do not banish me from your presence, and don't take your Holy Spirit from me. Restore to me again the joy of your salvation, and make me willing to obey you.

Psalm 51: 10-12 New Living Bible

In looking back over the difficult situation Betty, my husband and I faced with Nehemiah, we realized that the Lord had greater plans than we could have ever imagined. He had plans to give us a better future than we could have dreamed of; this is what is stated in the Bible. He has blessed us with more than we could have hoped or asked for. Both my husband and I, and our daughters were all transformed through this great trial that occurred in our lives. We have a greater peace and joy, as well as, a greater knowledge of the goodness of the Lord. What we did not realize, though, was that there were things in our own lives that the Lord needed to remove. All we could see in this problem with Nehemiah was our need to FIX HIM and life would be fine again. A vital key to keeping you "on track" throughout any difficult situation is to find out how you can change yourself. Search for a way that you can be transformed or at least changed in some area of your life in the midst of the problem.

I read a book called Change me, Oh Lord, by Evelyn Christenson, in which a mother was having many problems with her daughter. She decided to do something completely different from the usual way she dealt with her daughter in the past, which had only made her relationship with her daughter worse. She decided to stop criticizing and pointing out her daughter's faults for fourteen months. Instead, she stated positive things she saw in her daughter, and she decided to change her own self. Daily she asked the Lord to show her how she could change herself rather than her daughter. She would study the Bible, specifically the fruits of the spirit, which are: love, joy, peace, patience, kindness, goodness, faithfulness, gentleness, and self-control. Daily she asked the Lord to help her change. What she noticed was that her daughter started changing, without her mother doing the usual telling her daughter how she should change. In addition, she realized that as the Lord changed the mother, the things that her daughter did and said did not make her react in such a negative way. I highly recommend the book to encourage you to experience a different approach towards solving your problem.

This was her prayer:

"Lord, don't change Jan. (This is her daughter). I know she's a teenager who needs to find her way in the world. Just change me! Lord, make me that kind of mother You want me to be. O God, I know she's growing up. Show me, please, how you want me to change!"

She then began in earnest for 14 months of soul-searching for herself. She looked to the Bible for direction and began specifically in 1 Peter 3: 1-2. This Lord, Change Me, page 18 passage states:

"In the same way, you wives must accept the authority of your husbands, even those who refuse to accept the Good News. Your godly lives will speak to them better than any words. They will be won over by watching your pure, Godly behavior." Evelyn Christianson explains how the Lord showed her that, "Others were to observe my chaste and reverent behavior so that some … maybe won without a word."

She describes in her book, that this scripture was specifically speaking of a husband-and-wife relationship so that the spouse would be won over without a word but she applied this principle to work with her relationship with her daughter. She stated that she was, "Determined not to impose her philosophy on Jan again." No more "preachy mother!" Keeping her advice to herself especially with her personality wasn't easy."

As you begin this process of change, ask the Lord to change you, rather than doing it in your own strength. First, consider the importance of surrendering your fear, pride, and guilt. These are three of the enemy's favorite tools to use against you to leave you completely incapable of doing anything. Fear is torment. It is difficult to do anything when you are tormented. For further details, see the chapter on fear and guilt in the chapter entitled From Fear to Faith

My pride was the next barrier I needed to give up. I had to allow the Lord to change me. Let the Lord change you too. As you are able to reflect the image of Jesus in forgiving your son/daughter, loving them unconditionally, and yet showing tough love with firm rules, you will see changes occur in your child.

Although your child may be wrong about much of what has happened, you may need to say that you are sorry or "forgive me." This is a great way to break down any pride in either your child or yourself, thus, destroying a great barrier between you and your child. I was surprised to see the results.

Consider your heart now. The Lord commands us to forgive even if the person does not deserve it, just as we did not deserve to be forgiven when we accepted Jesus Christ as Lord of our lives. Have YOU forgiven your son or daughter? Stop now and consider this important question. Forgiveness can be a major block the enemy uses to keep you from having a mind filled with peace. Forgiveness has nothing to do with our emotions or how we feel about a person. It does not even matter if the person deserves it. Christ died for our sins when we did not deserve it. Forgiveness is an act of our will, which we choose to do in obedience to the Lord.

After forgiving the person, then we need to ask the Lord for His strength to complete the task. Remember though, forgiveness is an act of our will, not an emotion that feels good. Simply take the first step with your son or daughter to forgive them privately before the Lord. You may feel that you need to forgive them face to face, asking the Lord to give you the words and compassion. Let the Lord do the rest. You are not responsible for the results, only for your obedience to His commands. The following is a simple prayer that you can start with. Ask the Holy Spirit to lead you as you pray this prayer:

Preparation and Purification: Forgiveness Prayer

> *Lord Jesus, I ask you to forgive me for holding resentment toward others. By your grace, Lord God, I choose to forgive and release_____, (be specific) and I now place them into your hands. I choose to be obedient to you Lord, that if I forgive men their trespasses, our heavenly Father will also forgive me; if I do not forgive others, neither will I receive forgiveness. Therefore, I forgive all who have caused hurt in my life. (Pause and think of anyone that you need to forgive. Now forgive them by naming them aloud). I now ask you, God, to forgive me in every way I have sinned. I thank you that all these things are from you that you*

reconcile to me to yourself through Christ Jesus. I thank you and praise you that the reconciling power of the cross brings to me peace, rest and wholeness in this very hour as I have obeyed your command. (Adapted from Warfare Prayers For Prayer Warriors by Jan Wallens).

QUESTIONS

After reading this chapter, stop for a moment and consider what you have read. Now consider the following question and use the space to write out some of your feelings. How do I need to change?

STEP 4: FROM FEAR TO FAITH

Job answered GOD: 'I'm convinced: You can do anything and everything. Nothing and no one can upset your plans.' Job 42:1 The Message Bible Translation

For I cried to him and he answered me! He freed me from all my fears. Psalms 34:4 The Message Bible Translation

I will extol the LORD at all times; his praise will always be on my lips. My soul will boast in the LORD; let the afflicted hear and rejoice. Glorify the LORD with me; let us exalt his name together. I sought the LORD, and he answered me; he delivered me from all my fears. Those who look to him are radiant; their faces are never covered with shame. This poor man called, and the LORD heard him; he saved him out of all his troubles. The angel of the LORD encamps around those who fear him, and he delivers them. Taste and see that the LORD is good; blessed is the man who takes refuge in him. Fear the LORD, you his saints, for those who fear him lack nothing. The lions may grow weak and hungry, but those who seek the LORD lack no good thing. Come, my children, listen to me; I will teach you the fear of the LORD.

Whoever of you loves life and desires to see many good days, keep your tongue from evil and your lips from speaking lies. Turn from evil

and do good; seek peace and pursue it. The eyes of the LORD are on the righteous and his ears are attentive to their cry; the face of the LORD is against those who do evil, to cut off the memory of them from the earth. The righteous cry out, and the LORD hears them; he delivers them from all their troubles. The LORD is close to the brokenhearted and saves those who are crushed in spirit. A righteous man may have many troubles, but the LORD delivers him from them all; he protects all of his bones, not one of them will be broken. Evil will slay the wicked; the foes of the righteous will be condemned. The LORD redeems his servants; no one will be condemned who takes refuge in him. Psalm 34 New International Bible Version

This chapter's title from Fear to Faith is also the title of a great book written by Merlin Carothers which I highly recommend reading. Mr. Carothers' book explains how important it is to change our own perspective when viewing our difficulties and problems. Rather than focusing on our problems, we need to trust the Lord to help us. This is not an easy concept to understand. Culturally, we have been brought up to trust only what we can actually touch and see. The paradigm shift in our thinking is to change from being fearful of what we actually see, to believing in and trusting God to change what we actually do see. Faith is trusting in the Lord, not our circumstances.

What do you do if you feel fear? Many times, I felt a fear in my heart or terror of what was to come. I cried out to the Lord and He delivered me from all of my fears. The Lord would teach me what to do about this feeling. Sometimes, I would intercede with prayer for Nehemiah on my knees. I was amazed at what would happen. Once, we ended up unexpectedly seeing him when he "cut class" to go to a restaurant where he knew we would never go to eat. He never imagined that we would be able to find out what he was doing. And only God knows how many times he avoided further trouble and near death through the faithful prayers of our friends who stood "in the gap" for him.

Other times when I felt this fear, I would turn my mind to read the Bible, thinking about or speaking scriptures. See the chapter on The Word Never Returns Void. Calling a friend to pray with us was also very helpful. Sometimes, I was able to identify that this feeling of fear or terror was just meant to torment me. The Bible states that we need to let peace be our arbitrator. When we do not have peace, we need to go to the Lord and ask the Holy Spirit to help us. The Holy Spirit can reveal or uncover the truth so we can pray for a specific situation, or demonstrate to us that the fear resides in us, so that we can release it to the Lord.

Stop right now and ask the Holy Spirit to show you if there are any fears you need to give to Him. Is there something that is tormenting you? You can pray to the Lord just like you would talk to a friend about how you feel. Fear of failure as a mother is something that can get in the way of our relationship with our children and their growing up. As mothers, we can become so overbearing that we suffocate our children. Also fear of the unknown, or loss of control can be tormenting. If you cry out to the Lord, He can deliver you from all of your fears. You can call a friend to pray with you as I needed to do many times or you can go to a quiet place and allow the Holy Spirit to give you that peace that surpasses all understanding. Then the peace of the Lord will guard your heart and mind through Christ Jesus.

The fear of failing as a mother was very real to me, and I certainly thought that I was a failure. I constantly tried to figure out where I had gone wrong, so that I could change the situation with Nehemiah so I could help my friend Betty. I tried so hard to do everything perfectly so that life could be perfect. I heard a teaching by Christian woman which really helped me. She was teaching on the perfect father and I want to share it with you:

"Who was Adam's Father?" She asked.

"The Lord our God, of course..."

She said, "Did Adam have the perfect Father?"

"Well, yes," was the answer.

"Then why did Adam sin? It was his choice, wasn't it?"

She reminded me that Adam had a perfect Father who was God and a perfect environment, yet Adam chose to sin. Sometimes, people may have the correct environment with good parents teaching them correctly and lots of love, but they choose to sin. That short discourse set me free with abundant peace. I began to realize that I could depend on the Lord and forgive myself. For even the Lord our perfect Father had a son, Adam, who was not perfect. Adam sinned and changed the whole course of history. That was such a relief! I only wish that I had heard this many months before, so I could have given up the feelings of guilt, anguish, and thoughts that I was a failure as a mother.

Ask the Holy Spirit help you right now. Do you need to forgive yourself? The Lord already has. Let Him set you free today. This paradigm shift in your thinking is so important and yet so difficult to do. I recommend that you read the book by Merlin Carothers, *From Fear to FAITH.*" Also, T. D. Jakes has several tapes on faith that can help you with this paradigm shift.

He discusses how you can change your fears into faith and "faith your fear to death."

In order to renew your mind, you must fill it with the right message. The more you hear tapes like these and read books on this subject, as well as read the Bible, the quicker it can happen. This is the way to renew your mind by filling it with God's perspective on life. The renewing of your mind will affect your emotions, sleep, and everything and everyone around you.

QUESTIONS

Use this page to expose your deepest fears to the Lord, so He can set you free. Be honest with Him. He knows how you feel anyway.

STEP 5: PRAYER: BREAKING STRONGHOLDS

We are human, but we do not wage war with human plans and methods. We use God's mighty weapons, not mere worldly weapons, to knock down the Devil's strongholds. With these weapons we break down every proud argument that keeps people from knowing God. With these weapons we conquer their rebellious ideas, and we teach them to obey Christ. 2 Corinthians 10:3-5 New Living Bible Translation

In searching for answers that would help Nehemiah, I read many books in between driving to and from school and other activities. One book by Dutch Sheets, *"Intercessory Prayer,"* gave me great insight into why I felt like I was hitting a brick wall whenever Nehemiah and I were discussing any problems together. No amount of logical arguments or consequences for his actions seemed to change his attitude and behavior. Dutch Sheets calls this a stronghold or fortress surrounding a person's thoughts, which is explained in more detail in his book. I recommend that you read his book. In Dutch Sheets book, Intercessory Prayer, he explains how Satan or the devil, actually holds onto believers and nonbelievers' minds so that they are unable to hear the truth to be set free. This is a stronghold.

The word stronghold has its root meaning in Greek. According to Dutch Sheets, the definition in Greek for the word "stronghold" is a place from which to hold something strongly such as a castle or prison. In chapter ten called, "Most High Man", of the book Intercessory Prayer Dutch Sheets discusses how a person can be held captive by a stronghold. There are a multitude of factors causing a person to hold on to a belief as if it is surrounded by a fortress, even when the belief is false.

Have you ever tried to logically argue with someone about the Bible or a specific opinion? It seems like they "just don't get it" no matter how loud or convincing or perfectly logical your arguments are. This book gives some insight into this problem through Biblical analysis of the root of the words. He explains how to pray for people whether Christians or non-Christians who are held as "prisoners" or "captives" in certain areas of their thought patterns or opinions. Praying in these specific ways allows them to see the truth and be set free.

First of all, as we study the Bible it is clear that people are blind to the truth. In 1 Corinthians 3:14 the scripture states: *"But the natural man does not receive the things of the spirit of God, for they are foolishness to him; nor can he know them, because they are spiritually discerned."*

> 2 Corinthians 4:3 states: *"But even if our gospel is veiled, it is veiled to those who are perishing, whose minds the God of this age has blinded, who do not believe..."*

Therefore, we must have a plan to pray that the unbelievers can know the truth. Our plan begins with the study of 2 Corinthians 10:3-5 in The Living Bible. I have included two different translations of this scripture: *"It is true that I am an ordinary, weak human being, but I don't use human plans and methods to win my battles. I use God's mighty weapons, not those made by men, to knock down the devil's strongholds. These weapons can break down every proud argument against God and every wall that can be built to keep men from finding him. With these weapons I can capture rebels and bring them back to God and change them into men whose hearts' desire is obedience to Christ."*

The following is another translation of 2 Corinthians 10:3-5 from the New King James version: *"For though we walk in the flesh, we do not war according to the flesh. For the weapons of our warfare are not carnal but mighty in God for pulling down strongholds, casting down arguments and every high thing that exalts itself against the knowledge of God, bringing every thought into captivity to the obedience of Christ."*

The weapons that we have for the destruction of the fortress or stronghold are explained in verse 5. If you would like to know more about the root meanings and specific understanding of these words, I encourage you to read chapter ten in the book by Dutch Sheets. Generally speaking, the verse explains that we have powerful weapons we can use by applying the Word of God in order to see people change their ideas about God. It explains that we are in a war, a spiritual war in which we cannot use our "flesh" or natural way of thinking in order to change things. There are powerful weapons which can break up fortresses or strongholds keeping a person thinking a certain way.

The word of God can remove arguments or mindsets which influence a person's thoughts or actions. It can remove pride and anything that seems to place itself above God. And these weapons can "take a thought captive," or affect the thoughts that actually come into the mind of a person. According to Dutch Sheets, it is important to find out the strongholds of the person that you are praying for. "If you do not know what they are, then ask the Holy Spirit to reveal them to you. He will, and when He does, call them by name, according to 2 Corinthians 10:3-5. Speak, *"In the name of the Lord Jesus Christ I am destroying you, stronghold of_____."* Pray this daily until the person changes."

I have enclosed a portion of Dutch Sheets book. This is about a woman who has been praying for her brother Kevin for many years without any results. I hope this will give you encouragement regarding a great way to pray for somebody who needs to be saved.

"Marlena had been praying for her brother, Kevin, to be saved for approximately 12 years with no seeming results. She basically prayed things such as 'Lord, come into his life,' or 'Lord, reveal yourself to him.' As with many of us, she didn't realize that there were more specific Biblical ways to pray. Also, similar to the rest of us, she sometimes grew frustrated and tried to take things into her own hands saying things such as, 'You just need to give your life to the Lord'; or 'You have to quit doing this stuff you're doing.' Predictably, this would only result in her seeing the pride in rebellion in Kevin rise up, actually making things worse. 'Then I would really feel like I had blown it,' she said. 'Kevin was heading down a rocky road. He had major problems, including drugs, depression, and extreme anger,'" Marlena relates.

Early in 1995, she took a class of mine in which I taught these principles about praying for the lost. Marlena shared them with her husband, Patrick and their children. They began to pray the principles over Kevin. They specifically prayed the following (all per parenthetical remarks are mine):

- that God would lift the veil over him (revelation and enlightenment);
- for the Holy Spirit to hover over him and protect him;
- for godly people to be in his pathway each day;
- to cast down anything that would exalts itself against the knowledge of God, specifically pride and rebellion (this would include the huposoma aspect of the stronghold.);

- to take down all known strongholds-- thought patterns, opinions on religion, materialism, fear (this is the logismos dimension of the stronghold.);
- To bind Satan from taking Kevin captive; to bind all wicked thoughts and lies Satan would try to place in Kevin's mind (These would be the noema aspect of the stronghold.;
- That the armor of God would be placed on him.

After two weeks of praying in this way, Kevin overdosed on drugs and in his time of need cried out to God. "The Lord met him in a powerful way. The veil was definitely lifted and he had a revelation of God. He now has an understanding of the Word and responds to it. The confusion is gone! Kevin separated himself from the world and his former friends. He is now pursuing God and Christian relationships. His focus is on pleasing God, knowing him more and more. He is even considering missions. *"We know that we are of God, and the whole world lies in the power of the evil one."* (1 John 5:19).

> *"Yet we have been given authority! We can turn unbelievers "from darkness to light and from the dominion of Satan to God.* (Acts 26:18). *We are called to enforce and make effectual the freedom Christ procured."*

According to Dutch Sheets, "The unbeliever cannot war for himself. He cannot and will not overcome the strongholds of darkness, and he will not understand the gospel until the veil lifts. We must take our divinely dynamic weapons and fight. The powers of darkness will resist but *"do not be afraid of them; remember the Lord who is great and awesome, and fight for your brothers, your sons and daughters, your wives, and your houses."* (Nehemiah 4:14).

I hope that you are encouraged with the power of prayer and the specific application of the word of God to a difficult situation. Remember that Jesus said to him, "If you can believe, all things are possible to him who believes."

QUESTIONS

Use this page to write your specific prayer for your child in order To Fight the Enemy. Design a prayer focusing on correcting your child's weaknesses using the scripture. For example, in my weakness your strength (meaning the Lord's strength) is made perfect. Or if they are depressed, pray that the joy of the Lord is their strength.

STEP 6: PRAYER AND FASTING

"Is not this the kind of fasting I have chosen: to loose the chains of injustice and untie the cords of the yoke, to set the oppressed free and break every yoke? Is it not to share your food with the hungry and to provide the poor wanderer with shelter— when you see the naked, to clothe him, and not to turn away from your own flesh and blood?" Isaiah 58:6-7 New International Bible

A friend of ours, who has been a pastor for many years, gave me a tremendous book called, *"The Miracle Results of Fasting,"* by Dave Williams. It changed my life and my son's life. This is a short paperback book that can be read quickly, which I highly recommend reading; although I am sure you can find many other books on fasting. Our friends and pastor encouraged my husband and I to read it, in the battle for Nehemiah's life, and I believe that the gift of this book has contributed to Nehemiah being alive today. This chapter summarizes some of what I have learned through this book on fasting.

Many times, the scripture in Matthew 17:21 came to my mind: *"However, this kind does not go out except by prayer and fasting."* I was not quite sure what to do about this scripture, although I knew I needed to pray and fast for nehemiah, as I had never fasted before. I was not sure how long to fast, what kind of food to eat or abstain from, how to go about it: by myself, with a group, or where to begin. This book gave me some specific pointers in all of these areas. For this reason, I highly recommend that you read this book.

What is fasting all about anyway? Abstaining from food and using this time in prayer to the Lord is a fast. "Fasting humbles the soul before God, it denies and masters the appetite, it manifests an earnest desire to see God, it helps in giving us power over demonic oppression, and aids in prayer," according to Dave Williams.

My experience with fasting in general is that without opening my mouth to tell others how to fix themselves, people and circumstances began to change and improve following a fast. I felt that after the fast was over, I was able to see some progress in the right direction in situations that did not seem to be improving otherwise. It is amazing but very true that every time that I have been willing to fast, I would see significant changes occur.

There are many kinds of fasts. Some people fast and drink only water. They may do this for one day, three days or longer. Some people drink liquid protein, juices and water for one to three days or longer. In the book of the Bible, Daniel, it describes how Daniel ate "*no pleasant food.*" It is believed that he refrained from proteins and sugars, eating a diet of primarily fruits and vegetables. Everyone can be a participant in a fast regardless of their physical condition or daily work requirements. I have heard some people give up sugar, television, Nintendo games and a variety of other items for a specific timeframe. Some people can give up things that are important to them, as not everyone is able to go "on a water fast." (A "water fast" is when a person is drinking only water for a certain amount of time.) This way everyone can participate in one way or another.

You can pray and fast individually or corporately, for example: as a whole church, or as a family. We have also had great results when we prayed and fasted as a family, each member choosing something to give up for a period of time and for a specific purpose. I was thrilled to see each child give up something that I knew was important to them. One daughter gave up the computer and cell phone messages for a week, and I knew that talking to her friends was important using instant messenger. Let them choose what they believe they should give up to be a part of the family fast. Beware of the fact that fasting may make you feel a little miserable at first. Go slow.

I decided to give up breakfast for 21 days. During these 21 days, my husband and I would also fast our lunch and dinner on Fridays together. It was during this time that we: Betty, my husband or I would discover Nehemiah at places and doing things that we were very surprised to find out about. For example, we arrived in a restaurant where we encountered Nehemiah eating when he should have been at school. Also, his behavior improved. I believe that because we were fasting the Lord supernaturally kept him from danger and serious trouble as well as begin to make changes in him.

In the Bible, the book Daniel reveals the importance of praying with perseverance. Daniel prayed for 21 days. The scripture explains that his prayer was heard on the first day that he prayed, but because he persevered for the 21 days, it came to fruition. There was actually a spiritual battle going on during the 21 days that Daniel continued to pray. You can read more about this in the Bible book called Daniel, chapter 10.

I do not want you to think that there is a magical way to drink only water for a few days and guarantee that God will answer all of your prayers. However, I do believe that the Lord honors your heart and that there is something powerful in the combination of prayer and fasting. There is another aspect of fasting that is very important, which is our actions toward other people in general, and specifically while we are fasting. How are we treating others?

The Bible states in the book of Isaiah chapter 58: *"They love to make a show of coming to me and asking me to take action on their behalf. 'We have fasted before you!' they say. 'Why aren't you impressed? We have done much penance, and you don't even notice it!'" I will tell you why! It's because you are living for yourselves even while you are fasting. You keep right on oppressing your workers."*

"What good is fasting when you keep on fighting and quarreling? This kind of fasting will never get you anywhere with me. You humble yourselves by going through the motions of penance, bowing your head like a blade of grass in the wind. You dress in sackcloth and cover yourselves with ashes. Is this what you call fasting? Do you really think this will please the LORD?"

"No, the kind of fasting I want calls you to free those who are wrongly imprisoned and to stop oppressing those who work for you. Treat them fairly and give them what they earn. I want you to share our food with the hungry and to welcome poor wanderers into your homes. Give clothes to those who need them, and do not hide from relatives who need your help. "If you do these things, your salvation will come like the dawn. Yes, your healing will come quickly. Your godliness will lead you forward, and the glory of the LORD will protect you from behind. Then when you call, the LORD will answer."

In Dave William's book on page 88 and 89 different kinds of fasts are listed:

Plan A:

Fast completely for three days, drinking only distilled water. After that drink juices for a few days, and eat only fruits and vegetables for the remaining days. This is called a "Daniel fast."

Plan B:

Fast completely for seven days, drinking only distilled water. After that, drink juices for a few days, then follow the "Daniel fast" for the remainder of the days.

Plan C:

Fast one designated day per week for a whole year. That is 52 days per year.

Plan D:

Fast two designated days a week for a whole year. That is 140 days per year.

Plan E:

Fast three to seven days every three months, plus once a week.

Plan F:

Skip one or two meals on designated days each week.

Plan G:

Do a Daniel fast for as many days as God directs. I do not recommend to fast more than 40 days. This means consuming distilled water, juices, vegetables, and fruits only. Perhaps you can designate one day a week as your "meat day" and stay on the Daniel fast for the other days.

As I explained above, the Lord honors your heart. Please do not read over these ideas and feel that you are obligated to do any of these things in order to see the results you want. I recommend that you pray about whether and how you should fast. Share this with a friend, family member, or your pastor to make sure this is appropriate for you. You should also check with your doctor to obtain their opinion as to whether you are able to fast, and if so, what kind of fast is permissible.

Here are a few additional scriptures about fasting:

"So it was, when I heard these words that I sat down and wept, and mourned for many days; I was fasting and praying before the God of heaven." Nehemiah 1:4

"Now, therefore, says the Lord, turn to me with all your heart, with fasting, with weeping and with morning." Joel 2: 12

"But when you fast, put oil on your head and wash your face, 18 so that your fasting will not be noticed by others but by your Father who sees in secret. And your Father who is in secret will reward you." Mathew 6:17-18

QUESTIONS

In the space below, write down what kind of fast you may be led to try and the results that you are asking the Lord for.

CHAPTER 6

Out of Control-What Do I Do Now?

Solomon, the son of King David, now took firm control of the kingdom, for the LORD his God was with him and made him very powerful.

2 Chronicles 1:1 International Standard Bible

This chapter is written for the parent of a teenager who is completely out of control or on the way there. Your daughter or son may be in such rebellion that they do not want to go to school, come home at curfew time, speak politely with you, and may have been violent with you or threatened violence just in their demeaning manner. They do not want to do anything that you say. You have even considered calling the police. This teenager needs tough love. There are a variety of resources available just for you.

There are three books that I highly recommend reviewing. Dr. Dobson has written a book called, *"Tough Love,"* Dr. Henry Cloud has written a book called, *"Boundaries,"* and STEP (Systematic Training for Effective Parenting of Teens) has a book called, *"Parenting Teenager's."* At the end of this study, I have a page called references and recommended reading where you can find out how to obtain these books.

I have enclosed some of the ideas from these books. I recommend that you read them and study them for more information and help. One of the problems parents have when teenagers arrive at this level of rebellion is lack of preparation in knowing what to say and do in different situations. It is very important to be prepared in order to prevent the situation from escalating and becoming totally out of control. If you can memorize a few key phrases to answer your child with, this can make a difference in the results. This excerpt gives you some examples about how to answer your rebellious teenager in the heat of an argument.

For example: "I'm really sorry that this is difficult for you, but my answer is still no. I hope that you can understand because our relationship is very important to me."

Another great answer is: "How you respond to this is up to you. I can't control that. I do love you, but I still am serious about my limits."

In this excerpt from Dr. Cloud's book, he emphasizes the importance of the parent's responsibility for being loving and honest, but not responsible for the other person's reaction or response to the parent. The following are a few different ways to answer your child:

"You can make that choice if you desire. I can't do too much about that. But what I said is still true."

"I'm sorry that this is your response, but you are entitled to it. I still want you to know that I love you, but my answer is still the same."

"How you respond is up to you. I can't control that. I do love you, but I still am serious about my limits."

These references demonstrate a variety of approaches to deal with difficult adolescents. For example, the difference between their actions and your reactions to their actions is demonstrated in these answers to them. They use practical everyday situations and also an alternative is given. Children being held accountable for their actions and reaping the consequences is also described in a practical matter. Unconditional love for your children, regardless of their actions and showing appreciation for good behavior is very important. This is called tough love and it is very tough at times.

I have included a few pages from the book Systematic Training for Effective Parenting of Teens (STEP) called Parenting Teenager's. This scenario shows how you can set and use consequences with your teenager. Do not hesitate to set boundaries, require consequences to actions, and enforce your consequences. Also, if you need outside help, go to your family doctor, Pastor, or counselor. Every situation is different, but get help!

Parenting Teenagers or Systematic Training for Effective Parenting of Teens (Step) is well worth reading. In chapter five, consequences are addressed. Teenagers like to have some control and therefore consequences that allow choices are very helpful. The first question in chapter five, "How can I set and use consequences with my teenager?" The first step is to identify the goal. "When your teen misbehaves, use consequences. For the consequences to be effective, you first need to consider if the teenagers have a specific goal in mind with their misbehavior."

For example, is attention the desired result? "When a teen seeks attention it's best to avoid giving that attention on demand," according to STEP. The next possibility is power. "When a teen seeks power, the best consequence is having no one to fight with." The third possibility to look for is revenge. According to Step, teenagers can use items such as failing in school to get even with parents. "If your teen seeks revenge, use consequences instead of feeling hurt. They can help you focus on building respect and trust."

The second aspect of, "How can I set and use consequences with my teenagers," described by STEP is to decide who owns the problem or who is responsible for the problem. For example, if your teenager stayed up too late, he will be tired the next day. If your child misses the school bus, they will need to find another way to get to school. The way you react to these problems, determines if they own the problem with its consequences or you do. If you jump in and decide you can do their homework, so they don't need to stay up late at night, or give them an excuse to go to school late, so they can sleep in, then they don't learn the consequences of their behavior.

In these scenarios, you would actually appear to be the person responsible for the problem. Similarly, if you go to work late in order to help your daughter get to school because he or she missed the bus he/she hasn't learned to take responsibility for their own actions. "Job trading" was discussed by STEP as an additional way to use consequences and maintain the teen as the responsible person. If your teen failed to complete their chores around the house, then you can assign them an alternative job of yours. For example, if your son forgot to take the trash out, you can have him do some laundry, or water the plants, etc. as a method of exchange.

The third aspect of, "How can I set and use consequences with my teenager?" is to offer choices. I've always liked the idea of offering choices. My dad would often use this method to discipline us. He always picked the choices and we usually didn't really want to do either one, but found one choice we liked better. STEP uses these examples:

"Either pick up the things you left in the family room, or I'll put them in a box in the storage bin to get them out of the way."

"Either slow down, or stop the car and I'll drive."

"I'm willing to wash only the dirty clothes I find in the hamper."

This last idea I have used with my own children, stating as follows: "I will wash all the clothes that I find in the hamper." It worked very well to get the dirty clothes off the floor and into the hamper. This is not an exact science, or drama that you can memorize in order to replay at any moment. Rather it is a better way of dealing with problems that can be very aggravating and do not need to be the center of attention.

I personally felt better after giving choices and consequences to our children, like washing only dirty clothes in the hamper. The underlying anger and aggravation can be removed from a situation in this manner. The follow-through is the most important part of using consequences and choices with your teenager. Make sure that you are willing to enforce your follow-through before you give a consequence. If you say they have to take out the trash or they don't go to the party on Friday night, then you are obligated to check up on them. If they do not take the trash out, then they cannot go to the party on Friday. It sounds simple, but it can be very difficult. If your son or daughter is not always responsible, then you will need to check and make sure that the trash has been taken out. By following through you can then give permission for your son or daughter to attend the party.

STEP also points out that, "If your teen chooses a consequence, the decision has to stand for the moment." This emphasizes to them the importance of being responsible and following through. They know they can count on consequences which they do not like if they do not obey. This is a great way to get them ready for the real-world. One day they will have a boss and do a number of things they do not want to do. STEP gives some guidelines for using consequences which are pretty straightforward but worth reviewing. Many times, after months of discord, Betty and I had felt angry and it was difficult to continue in a positive way and with unconditional love.

The following guidelines are used to reinforce the kind of behavior that we truly want to display, regardless of how we feel:

1. Be both firm and kind.
2. Talk less and act more.
3. Don't fight or give in.
4. Use respectful words.
5. Make it clear when there isn't a choice.
6. Focus on positive behavior.
7. Do not worry about what others think.
8. Stay calm.
9. Respect the other parent or parents.
10. Be patient

QUESTIONS

How can you help your child become responsible and accept consequences for their choices? How will you follow through?

CHAPTER 7

The Word Never Returns Void

The Word Never Returns Void. It is the same with my word. I send it out, and it always produces fruit. It will accomplish all I want it to, and it will prosper everywhere I send it.

Isaiah 55:11 New Living Bible

The Bible is a living book that can be used and applied to today's problems. The spoken scriptures of the Bible over your situation have a great effect on your circumstances. In the Bible, it states that the, "*word never returns void but goes forth to accomplish what it was sent to do.*" Although it may sound a little strange to you right now, in studying the scriptures and understanding them there is a very important concept for you to understand. We can stand on a promise from the scriptures by speaking out loud and believing that for our children.

I Corinthians in the Bible states that we can speak those things that are not as if they were. This is faith! Trusting that the Lord will fulfill his word, or cause this to happen. Of course, we need to be diligent in our responsibilities as well. Maybe you are thinking that this could never happen. I can't speak to things and have them appear. Speaking the scriptures is certainly not the magical potion which will cause the genie to jump out of the bottle and immediately solve your problems. I do not intend to imply this. Also, we do have to be patient and trust the Lord to answer our prayers in His perfect timing. (And sometimes with a better/different plan than we asked for or desired.)

Now, you can choose to ignore this idea that our words, when aligned with the Bible, can change the circumstances. Einstein stated that the definition of insanity is doing the same thing over and over and expecting a different result. If your way wasn't working, try the Lord's way. Also, the importance of our everyday words regarding our problems and situations is very powerful. The scriptures states that "the power of life and death is in the tongue. *"The tongue has the power of life and death, and those who love it will eat its fruit."* Proverbs 18:21

Therefore, I encourage you to speak the Word over your children. I suggest that you bring these scriptures with you wherever you go. You can put them in your pocket. Do not speak your fears all day. Share your feelings with your friends, but speak the scriptures from the Bible, the powerful Word of God, in order to change the circumstances. Your fears and anxieties do not change the circumstances.

I recommend that you choose some of the following scriptures that best pertain to your situation to study daily as well as speak out loud. You can put on a 3 by 5 card and carry around in your pocket too:

I pray that my son/daughter_____ will be sober and vigilant, because his/her adversary the devil walks about like a roaring lion, seeking whom he may be devour. I pray that he/she will resist him, steadfast in the faith, knowing that the same sufferings are experienced by other Christians in the world. Revised from 1 Peter 5:8 –9 KJV Bible

I pray that my son/daughter_____ will submit to you, God, and that he/she will resist the devil and he will flee from her. Revised from James 4:7 KJV Bible

I pray that you, God have delivered my son/daughter _____ from the power of darkness and conveyed his/ her into the kingdom of Jesus, in whom he/she has redemption through his blood, the forgiveness of sin. Colossians 1:13 -- 14 Revised from Colossians 1:13 KJV Bible

I pray that in all things my son/daughter _____ is more than a conqueror through Him who loves his/her. Revised from Romans 8:37 KJV Bible

I pray, God, that the accuser of my son's/ daughter's _____, who accuses his/her before her God day and night, has been cast down. I pray that he/ she overcame him by the blood of the lamb and by the word of his/her testimony. Revised from Revelations 12:10-11 KJV Bible

I pray that neither death nor life, nor angels nor principalities nor powers nor things present nor things to come, nor height nor depth, or any other created thing, shall be able to separate my son/daughter _____ from the love of God which is in Christ Jesus his/her Lord. Revised from Romans 8:38-39 KJV Bible

I pray that though my son/daughter _____ walks in the flesh, he/she does not war according to the flesh. For the weapons of his/her warfare are not carnal but mighty in God for the pulling down strongholds, casting down arguments and every high thing that exalts itself against the knowledge of

God, bringing every thought to the obedience of Christ. Revised from 2 Corinthians 10:3—54 KJV Bible

I pray that my son/daughter _____ *has her senses exercised to discern both good and evil.* Revised from Hebrews 5:14 KJV Bible

I pray, Lord, that you will guard my son/daughter _____ *from the evil one.* Revised from 2 Thessalonians 3:3 KJV Bible

I pray, God, that your presence will go with my son/daughter _____ *forever.* Revised from Exodus 33:14 KJV Bible

I pray, God, that my son/daughter _____ *will be strong and of good courage; that he/she will not be afraid, nor dismayed, for you, the Lord his/her God, are with him/ her wherever he/she goes.* Revised from Joshua 1:9 KJV Bible

I pray, God, that you will preserve the soul of my son/daughter _____ *and that you will deliver him/her out of the hands of the wicked.* Revised from Psalm 97: 10 KJV Bible

I pray, God, that you are my son's/daughter's _____ *refuge and that you will thrust out the enemy from before him/her.* Revised from Deuteronomy 33:27 KJV Bible

I pray, God, that the angel of the Lord encamps all around my son/daughter who fears you, and delivers him/her. Revised from Psalms 34:7 KJV Bible

I pray that Satan will not take advantage of my son/daughter _____ *for he/she is not ignorant of his devices.* Revised from 2 Corinthians 2:11 KJV Bible

I pray that my son/daughter_____ knows that he/she does not live by bread alone but by every word that proceeds from the mouth of God. Revised from Matthew 4:4 KJV Bible

I pray, Lord, that my son/daughter _____ will drive Satan away by worshiping the Lord God, and Him only he/she shall serve. Revised from Matthew 4:10 KJV Bible

I pray that my son/daughter _____ will gird up the loins of his/her mind and be sober, and rest his/her hopefully upon the grace that is to be brought to him/her at the revelation of Jesus Christ as an obedient child, not conforming himself/herself to the former lusts, as in his/her ignorance, but as you, God called his/her are holy, may he/ she also be Holy in all his/ her conduct. Revised from 1 Peter 1:13 –15 KJV Bible

I pray that my son /daughter _____will have the mind of Christ. Revised from 1 Corinthians 2:16 KJV Bible

I pray that you, God, will open my son's/daughter's _____ eyes, in order to turn them from darkness to light, and from the power of Satan to you, that she may receive forgiveness of sins and an inheritance among those who are sanctified by faith in Jesus. Revised from Acts 26:18 KJV Bible

I pray God that you preserve the soul of my son/ daughter_____ and deliver his/her out of other hand of the wicked. Revised from Psalms 97: 10 KJV Bible

I pray, God, for my son/daughter_____ that the son of God was manifested that he might destroy the works of the devil. Revised from 1 John 3:8 KJV Bible

I pray for my son/daughter_____ that he/she puts off, concerning her former conduct, the old man which grows corrupt according to the deceitful lusts, and be renewed in the spirit of his/her mind and that he/she put on the new man which was created according to you, God, in true righteousness and Holiness. E Revised from ph. 4:22 – 24 KJV Bible

I pray that my son/daughter_____ is strong, and that the word of God abides in him/her and he/she has overcome the wicked one. 1 Revised from John 2:14 KJV Bible

I do not pray, God, that you should take my son/daughter _____out of the world, but that you should keep him/her from the evil one. Revised from John 17:15 KJV Bible

I pray that my son/daughter_____ will not give place to the devil. Revised from Eph. 4:27 KJV Bible Adapted from Praying God's Will for My Daughter, by Lee Roberts.

QUESTIONS

My personal list of specific scriptures for my children are:

CHAPTER 8

Prayer That Moves Mountains

Jesus was matter-of-fact: *"Embrace this God-life. Really embrace it, and nothing will be too much for you. This mountain, for instance: Just say, 'Go jump in the lake'—no shuffling or shillyshallying— and it's as good as done. That's why I urge you to pray for absolutely everything, ranging from small to large. Include everything as you embrace this God-life, and you'll get God's everything. And when you assume the posture of prayer, remember that it's not all asking. If you have anything against someone, forgive—only then will your heavenly Father be inclined to also wipe your slate clean of sins."*

Mark 11:20 The Message Bible Translation

PRAYER OF SALVATION

This prayer is for someone who has never given their life to the Lord. Do not spend one more day without the Lord. The Lord can be your best friend accompanying you in everyday activities, encouraging you and never leaving you. Repeat this prayer out loud and then call someone who is a Christian to help you with your new life:

"Dear God, I confess that I have sinned against you in so many ways. I bring these before you _____ (name any sin that you can think of). Please forgive me for these sins. I accept your forgiveness for these sins. Jesus, I ask you now to come and take control of my life. I will do whatever you tell me to. Help me to turn away from my sins and to follow you. I accept your free gift of eternal life. I know that I am not worthy of it, but I thank you for it. Please fill me with the Holy Spirit now and give me grace so I can keep these promises. Amen." Adapted from the Ministry Training Manual by Randy Clark.

PRAYER: FOR GOD'S BATTLE STRATEGY

Be strong in the Lord and in the power of his might. Put on the whole armor of God, that you will be able to stand against the wiles of the devil. For we wrestle not against flesh and blood, but against principalities, against Powers, against the rulers of the darkness of this world, against principal wickedness in high places. Wherefore take unto you the whole armor of God, that you will be able to withstand in the evil day, and having done all, to stand. Eph. 6:10 –13 KJV Bible

God tells us in the above scriptures that we enter into battle not on our own strength but with His strength. God has given us His power and His might through Jesus Christ. God tells us we battle do not battle against men and women, but we battle against the devil's army, against the powers of darkness. We put on God's armor using the sword which is the Bible to speak over situations and then the enemy must flee. Part of the armor of the Lord is the helmet of salvation which gives us Christ's mind and His thoughts. The shield of unwavering faith, another part of armor removes every mountain, every obstacle in our way. The belt of truth, another part of the armor allows no door of deception to be opened to us by the enemy. With God's sword, speaking the word of God which is the Bible over our situations we pierce the darkness with the truth.

PRAYER: EVERY YOKE BROKEN

Father, in Jesus name I thank you that every yoke the enemy has put on _____ (be specific) is now being destroyed. I rebuke Satan, binding his forces of darkness assigned against_____ (be specific). I thank you, Lord, that as your light shines through, and all blindness must leave in Jesus name. I now lose them from the enemy's powers and plans, declaring God is our shield, our refuge and high tower of safety. Holy Spirit, let your fires of revival spread like a wildfire within them. Lord, don't stop until eyes are opened and ears hear your truth. Ignite their spirit with yourself, Holy Spirit. Let change and transformation to the likeness of Christ now become a reality. Let repentance, surrender, and obedience come and a hunger and thirst for righteousness. Lord, let a desire to hear your voice and fulfill your destiny. In Jesus name. Amen. (Adapted from Warfare Prayers for Prayer Warriors by Jan Wallens)

PRAYER: THE BLOOD OF JESUS

In the name of Jesus Christ, I now apply the blood of Jesus over myself and all my family and _____, (the specific). I apply the sanctifying and redeeming blood of Jesus over every area of our lives. The blood Jesus brought defeat to Satan on Calgary, and I declare all power and authority over him and command Satan and all his spirits of darkness to leave now in Jesus name. I draw the blood-line of Jesus Christ around us _____ (name your family) and declare no evil can cross that blood line in Jesus name. In faith believing, in obedience and reverence, the blood Jesus has been applied and His victory belongs to us now in Jesus name, for the glory of God. For we have not been redeemed with corruptible things but with the precious blood of Christ. Amen. 1 Peter 1:18 –19 KJV Bible

PRAYER: SET THE CHILDREN FREE

Heavenly Father,

We thank you for the authority that was given to us by Jesus. Your words declare that whatever we bind on earth will be bound in heaven and whatever we release on earth will be released in heaven. On this day, therefore, we declare together and we say to the spiritual pharaoh who was held captive and is trying to hold captive our children -- -- to release them and to let them go!

We expose all the lies that you are throwing to them and we speak truth and light to the situations that they are facing. We thwart all his future plans against them and even now we

declare these plans and strategies to be null and void. We thank you for the power of the blood of Jesus shed at Calvary. For His blood is sufficient to break any curses, vices, lies and all other negative forces that have come and are coming against our children. We declare Christ's victory to all our children. We speak God's freedom upon them. We know that they will be victors in Christ for we know that you O Lord, will honor our prayers and grant of the desires of our hearts which is to see our children enter into the place and walk into the destiny which you have prepared for them. We release each one of our children to your care for as much as we love them, we know that you loved them more. Thank you, Father, for the great and mighty works that will be birthed into each of our children's lives. All these we speak in Jesus Christ's authority and name. Amen! Adapted from Warfare Prayers for Prayer Warriors by Jan Wallens

QUESTIONS

Make a list of God's promises to you now in this situation—This is your help!

RECOMMENDED READING AND REFERENCES

Most of these books are available at your local Christian bookstore unless otherwise specified.

1. Boundaries by Henry Cloud.
2. Breaking Generational Curses by Marilyn Hickey.
3. Change Me, Oh Lord by Evelyn Christenson.
4. From Fear to Faith, by Merlin Carothers.
5. Intercessory Prayer by Dutch Sheets.
6. Industry Training Manual by Randy Clark. 917-920-1345. Global Awakening Publishing.
7. Parenting Teenagers by American Guidance Service or STEP (Systematic Training for Effective Parenting of Teens) 800 328 2560 or www.agsnet.com.
8. Power of a Praying Parent by Stormie Omartian.
9. Ridding your home of spiritual darkness by Chuck Pierce.
10. The Miracle Results of Fasting by Dave Williams.
11. To Deliver Us from Evil by Cindy Jacobs.
12. Warfare Prayers for Prayer Warriors by Jan Wallens.
13. Prayers That Avail Much by Germaine Copeland.
14. Praying God's Will for My Daughter, by Lee Roberts.

BIOGRAPHY OF MICHELLE VERA, M.D.

GOD, my shepherd! I don't need a thing. You have bedded me down in lush meadows, you find me quiet pools to drink from. True to your word, you let me catch my breath and send me in the right direction. Even when the way goes through Death Valley, I'm not afraid when you walk at my side. Your trusty shepherd's crook makes me feel secure. You serve me a six-course dinner right in front of my enemies. You revive my drooping head; my cup brims with blessing. Your beauty and love chase after me every day of my life. I'm back home in the house of GOD for the rest of my life.

Psalm 23 The Living Bible

My name is Dr. Michelle Vera. I grew up near Los Angeles, California as the eldest of four children. My mother had a doctorate in Psychology and my father was a computer engineer. I attended college at the University of California, San Diego where I received my Bachelor's degree in Biology. I then completed my medical school degree in Puerto Rico, becoming bilingual in English and Spanish. It was during medical school that I rededicated my life to the Lord and desired to use my talents to serve Him.

I am happily married to a wonderful man who is a doctor specializing in Obstetrics and Gynecology. We have three children and 5 grandchildren. I enjoy reading, exercising, playing tennis, swimming, and most of all spending time with my family. I have worked as a physician at a variety of different office settings from private practice to large HMO's. I also worked in a rural health center where I treated migrant workers in order to repay the government for my medical education through the National Health Service Corporation program.

My life changed suddenly in April 1997, when I discovered my best friend's son in his room passed out after drinking alcohol with some friends, and I had to drive him to the emergency room. I began to look for a way to help him overcome this problem, despite his strong opposition. After I saw the tremendous change in him, from being a difficult teenager drinking alcohol totally out of control, to a football player for Alabama State University, I decided to write this book. I hope to help encourage other parents who are looking for answers for their troubled teenagers. There is help!

Made in the USA
Columbia, SC
17 January 2020